AF575354

Faustina

A Saint's Story for Children

Written by
Kaitlyn C. Mason

Illustrated by
Braelyn Snow

TAN Books
Gastonia, North Carolina

Illustrations by Braelyn Snow

Cover Design and Interior Layout by Jordan Avery

ISBN: 978-1-5051-2243-5
Kindle ISBN: 978-1-5051-2244-2
ePUB ISBN: 978-1-5051-2245-9

Published in the United States by
TAN Books
PO Box 269
Gastonia, NC 28053
www.TANBooks.com

Printed in India

From the Author

We are raising children in difficult times, but where sin abounds, grace abounds all the more (see Rom 5:20)! God wants us to run to His mercy and to lead others there too. That's the message Jesus gave to Saint Faustina. It's an important message for our times, and it's the message at the heart of this book. I love Saint Faustina because she never gave up. She knew what it was like to face rejection, ridicule, and deep suffering, but she also knew how to surrender everything to Jesus. That's something I strive to do every day in my own life, and it's something that I want my children to learn to do too. It is my hope that this story of the precious life of Saint Faustina can enrich your discussions with your own children, and that it will encourage your family to always trust in Jesus. God bless you!

In a simple house of white stone, the Kowalska family lived and thrived.
They were overjoyed to welcome baby Helen, in the year 1905.

Little Helen gathered eggs and led cows to pasture.
Hoping to get to Mass, she did her chores fast and faster.

The Mass Helen cherished, but hopes of going often perished.
The family owned too few nice gowns, for all the sisters to go to town.

Helen served God in other ways, collecting money for the poor.
She begged for alms from those she met, walking door to door.

Her father rose early to sing for Mary, his joyful songs filling the air.
He woke the family before the sun, but of their complaints, he did not care.

For Helen, the convent was her call, but her father would not consent at all.
Like him, she loved Jesus and Mary too! But still there was work she had yet to do.

Helen worked as a domestic, making homes look quite majestic.

She cared for babies and children too, telling them stories

and tying their shoes.

Then one night, at a dance, Jesus appeared in a vision. Would Helen become a nun? She needed to make a decision.

"How long will you keep putting me off?" Jesus asked, His tone quite bold.
Helen rushed to adoration, His presence more precious than gold.

She sought a convent without delay, knowing God would show the way.
But every one cast her aside, yet still she trusted and took it in stride.

Finally, the Sisters of Our Lady of Mercy accepted her petition.
As a novice, she would begin her divine mission.
She took her vows; she took her name; Maria Faustina's heart was set aflame.

As a porter, she opened the door.

She passed out food and loved the poor.

She chopped in the kitchen

and weeded in the garden.

She frequented confession to receive God's pardon.

In the bakery, she would never grumble. She did her duties, always humble.
But others found her job too draining. They took her place, ever complaining.

Faustina fell sick but kept on serving. Of love from Jesus, she felt undeserving. But she began to hear Him and to see His face. The suffering that followed she chose to embrace. Faustina accepted her every cross so that many souls would not be lost.

Her confessor asked her to keep a diary. She would write what Jesus told her, to help us know and come to see that our pain He would shoulder.

When a pot of potatoes she struggled to carry, she did her best, saying yes like Mary.
Then she saw, with great surprise, the potatoes turned to roses before her eyes!

Then one night while in her cell, she prayed on bended knee. Jesus told her, "Paint an image according to what you see." Jesus came closer, out of the night, each ray of mercy a beam of light. Red for the blood on the cross He spent, white for water to wash us when we repent.

But Faustina had neither skill nor talent to put the image in paint. This request from Jesus made her cry; she thought she might even faint! An artist was hired; he did his best, but Faustina claimed he could not pass the test.

She cried to Jesus, "Who will paint You as beautiful as You are?" Capturing His likeness was like capturing a star. Then He came just as before, standing before her face. "Not in the beauty of the color, nor of the brush lies the greatness of this image, but in My grace."

She finally accepted the artist's depiction, but it was not done, it needed an inscription. The words were written, "Jesus, I trust in You!" It was a phrase Faustina lived; it was a phrase Faustina knew.

The Divine Mercy Image spread far and wide to homes and churches between the tides. Yet Faustina had more work to do. Of those who loved Jesus, there were too few.

Faustina established a strong devotion; she set a movement of mercy in motion. An hour, a feast, a chaplet, a novena, we all received through Maria Faustina.

When we remember at the hour of three, that Jesus died on the cross, we pray the Divine Mercy Chaplet, knowing no prayer is lost.

God revealed the depths of His mercy to remind the whole world He cares. Never forget, dear children, that He always hears your prayers. We must run swiftly back to Him, before our time on earth is through. Trusting is hard, but mercy overflows when we pray, "Jesus, I trust in You!"

How to Pray the Chaplet of Divine Mercy

Jesus told Saint Faustina, "As often as you hear the clock strike the third hour, immerse yourself completely in My mercy, adoring and glorifying it; invoke its omnipotence for the whole world. . . . In this hour you can obtain everything for yourself and for others simply for the asking" (Diary, 1572).

The Chaplet of Divine Mercy is one of the special prayers that Jesus taught Saint Faustina. She recorded it in her diary and passed it on to all of us. Pray this as often as you can with your family, especially daily at 3:00 pm or on Fridays, and during Holy Week and on Divine Mercy Sunday (the Sunday following Easter).

Using rosary beads, start by making the sign of the cross,
then pray three times:
"O Blood and Water, which gushed forth from the Heart of Jesus as a fountain of mercy for us, I trust in You."

Then, on the first three beads, pray one Our Father, one Hail Mary, and the Apostles Creed.

For each Our Father bead, say:
"Eternal Father, I offer You the Body and Blood, Soul and Divinity of Your dearly beloved Son, Our Lord Jesus Christ, in atonement for our sins and those of the whole world."

For each of the ten Hail Mary Beads, say:
"For the sake of His sorrowful Passion, have mercy on us and on the whole world."

Repeat for each of the five decades of the rosary, and conclude by praying the following prayer three times:
"Holy God, Holy Mighty One, Holy Immortal One, have mercy on us and on the whole world."

Questions for Family Discussion

1. Saint Faustina was rejected from many convents before finally being accepted at the Sisters of Our Lady of Mercy. Can you think of a time when you felt rejected? Were you able to trust that God had a plan for your life the way Saint Faustina did? What did you do?

2. Saint Faustina carried out many different tasks to help out around her convent, and she did her best to perform them joyfully for Jesus, even when she was ill. What are some of the ways in which she served? What tasks or chores do you do at home to help your family? Is there anything you could do differently to serve a bit more joyfully for Jesus in these roles?

3. Saint Faustina was sometimes ridiculed for her faith. Have you ever experienced someone making fun of you or treating you unkindly? How can we pray for those who hurt us? What can we do to help them?

4. This book explains how the Divine Mercy image and message spread far and wide. Has it spread to your home yet? Have you ever seen the Divine Mercy image before? If so, where? What does this image express to humanity, and why might God have wanted us to have it in the world now?

5. Faustina chooses to honor Jesus through carrying out her daily tasks with joy, but also when she attends adoration, Mass, and confession. What are some special ways in which we can honor Jesus every day at 3:00 pm, the hour when He died on the cross for our salvation?

An Invitation to Trust Jesus

Here is a pledge through which you can make a commitment to place your trust in God.

I ______________________, choose to follow the example of Saint Faustina by doing my best to always run to Jesus. In times of joy, complacency, and sorrow, I will always strive to place all of my trust in Him and in His good plans for my life. He is the source of all my hope.

Signed: ______________________________

Date: _______________________

"Trust in the LORD with all your heart, and do not rely on your own insight. In all your ways acknowledge him, and he will make straight your paths."

—Proverbs 3:5–6

About the Author

Kaitlyn C. Mason is an author, speaker, and homeschooling mother of six helping her family reclaim their heritage and build up their homestead in rural Kentucky. She is co-founder of Mary Garden Showers, a national Catholic baby shower ministry sharing mercy with women and families experiencing crisis pregnancies. She is also a contributing author to *Our Friend Faustina* from Marian Press. Kaitlyn enjoys teaching French and learning Irish fiddle alongside her children. She writes to help you live simply and mercifully, so you can pursue and embrace the life you're called to live. Learn more at themercifulhome.com and marygardenshowers.org.

About the Illustrator

Braelyn Snow is an artist based out of Savannah, Georgia. Catholic sacred art is her primary artistic passion. She had the joy of working in the field of ecclesiastical interiors for several years at a fine art studio in Savannah. She also teaches visual arts with her students at a classical Christian school. She enjoys singing chant and sacred polyphony, photography, and thrifting for vintage clothing when she is not illustrating.